If you are what you eat...
than I'm

Fast,
Cheap
&
Easy

Cooking Thai

D1248525

Printed in the United States of America
by G&R Publishing Co.

Distributed By:

507 Industrial Street
Waverly, IA 50677

ISBN-13: 978-1-56383-246-8
ISBN-10: 1-56383-246-1
Item #7017

Table of Contents

Fast

Fast Main Dishes.......... 2
Fast Side Dishes 18
Fast Appetizers 33
Fast Desserts............... 36

Cheap

Cheap Main Dishes 42
Cheap Side Dishes 59
Cheap Appetizers 70
Cheap Desserts........... 74

Easy

Easy Main Dishes....... 82
Easy Side Dishes...... 103
Easy Appetizers........ 113
Easy Desserts 117

Index

Index 121

Fast

Tasty Thai Noodles and Shrimp

1 (32 oz.) container
  chicken broth
1 T. Thai seasoning
4 oz. thin rice noodles
1½ lb. uncooked shrimp,
  shelled and deveined

¼ C. fresh lime juice
2 green onions,
  thinly sliced
Lime wedges, optional

In medium saucepan over high heat, bring chicken broth, Thai seasoning and 2 cups water to a boil. Add thin rice noodles and uncooked shrimp to the chicken broth mixture. Continue to boil. Stir in lime juice and sliced green onions and cook until heated throughout. Spoon noodles and shrimp onto individual plates. Garnish each serving with a lime, if desired.

Garbanzo Beans and Couscous

1 (5.6 oz) box
   couscous with toasted
   pine nuts, uncooked
⅓ C. raisins
1 T. olive oil
1 medium zucchini,
   cut into ½″ pieces
1 clove garlic, crushed
¾ tsp. ground cumin

¾ tsp. ground coriander
⅛ tsp. cayenne pepper
2 (15 oz.) cans
   garbanzo beans,
   rinsed and drained
½ C. olives
Fresh parsley
   sprigs, optional

In a medium saucepan over high heat, bring 6 cups water to a boil. Add couscous and raisins to the water and prepare according to the directions on the package. In a 12″ skillet over medium high heat, heat olive oil. Add zucchini pieces to olive oil and cook for 5 minutes, stirring occasionally. Add garlic, cumin, coriander and pepper to zucchini and cook for 30 seconds, stirring occasionally. Add drained beans, olives and ¼ cup water to mixture and cook for an additional 5 minutes until heated throughout, stirring often. Add cooked couscous to bean mixture and toss gently. Spoon into individual serving bowls and garnish with fresh parsley sprigs, if desired.

Pork BBQ

1 (1 lb.) container fully
cooked shredded pork
in barbecue sauce

1 (15 oz.) can red
kidney beans, rinsed
and drained

1 (15 oz.) can black beans,
rinsed and drained

2 large plum
tomatoes, chopped

Buns

In medium saucepan over medium high heat, mix shredded pork, red beans, black beans, chopped tomatoes and 1 cup water. Bring the mixture to a boil. Reduce heat to low, cover saucepan and let simmer for 5 minutes to blend flavors, stirring occasionally. Spoon shredded pork onto buns and serve.

"Life moves pretty fast.
If you don't stop and look around
once in awhile, you could miss it."
~Ferris Bueller~

Fast Chicken Fettuccine

1 (9 oz.) pkg. refrigerated red sweet pepper fettuccine pasta
¼ C. sun-dried tomatoes in oil
2 C. sliced zucchini

½ lb. skinless, boneless chicken breast strips
½ C. finely grated Parmesan, Romano or Asiago cheese
Pepper to taste

Using kitchen scissors, cut fettuccine pasta in half. According to package directions, in a medium saucepan, boil fettuccine in lightly salted water. Drain fettuccine and return to hot pan. Drain sun-dried tomatoes, reserving 2 tablespoons oil from jar. In a large skillet over medium-high heat, warm 1 tablespoon reserved oil. Add zucchini to the oil and cook and stir for 2 to 3 minutes or until crisp-tender. Remove zucchini from skillet. Add remaining reserved oil to skillet. Cook chicken in the oil for 2 to 3 minutes or until no longer pink. Mix zucchini, chicken, tomato strips and grated cheese with cooked fettuccine and toss gently to combine. Season with pepper to taste.

Speedy Sausage and Beans

¾ lb. bulk hot or mild
  Italian sausage
1½ C. chopped onion
1 tsp. ground cinnamon
¼ tsp. ground allspice
2 C. water

1 (15 oz.) can dark red
  kidney beans, rinsed
  and drained
⅓ C. raisins
1 (14½ oz.) can diced
  tomatoes, drained

In a large saucepan over medium high heat, cook sausage and onion until sausage is no longer pink. Drain the sausage and onion. Stir in cinnamon and allspice and cook for 1 minute. Stir in water, kidney beans and raisins. Bring mixture to a boil and reduce heat. Cover saucepan and let simmer for 15 minutes. Stir in drained tomatoes and cook until heated throughout.

Tangy Dinner Steaks

1 T. Dijon mustard
4 beef tenderloin steaks
2 T. olive oil
2 (4 oz.) pkgs.
   sliced mushrooms

⅓ C. dry red wine or sherry
1 T. Worcestershire sauce
2 tsp. fresh chopped thyme
½ C. beef broth
1 tsp. cornstarch

Spread mustard evenly over both sides of steaks. In a large skillet over medium heat, warm 1 tablespoon olive oil. Add steaks to oil and cook to desired doneness, turning once. Transfer steaks to a serving platter. Keep warm. Add remaining oil to skillet. Add mushrooms to skillet, cook and stir for 4 minutes. Stir in dry wine or sherry, Worcestershire sauce and thyme. Simmer, uncovered, for 3 minutes. In a small bowl, combine beef broth and cornstarch. Stir cornstarch mixture into mushroom mixture. Cook and stir until thickened and bubbly. Cook and stir for an additional 2 minutes. Spoon the mixture over each steak and serve.

Curried Chicken Soup

5 C. water
1 (3 oz.) pkg. chicken-
  flavored ramen noodles
2 tsp. curry powder
1 C. sliced fresh
  mushrooms

2 C. cubed cooked
  turkey or chicken
1 medium apple, cored
  and coarsely chopped
½ C. canned sliced
  water chestnuts

In a large saucepan, combine water, flavoring packet from noodles and curry powder. Bring to a boil. Break up ramen noodles. Add ramen noodles and mushrooms to mixture in saucepan. Reduce heat. Simmer noodles, uncovered, for 3 minutes. Stir in cubed turkey or chicken, chopped apple and water chestnuts. Cook until heated throughout.

Sweet Sesame Chicken Kabob Salad

4 skinless, boneless
  chicken breast halves

2 T. vegetable oil

3 T. white wine vinegar

1 T. sesame seed oil

1 T. soy sauce

½ tsp. dry mustard

¼ tsp. crushed red pepper

1 T. bottled plum sauce
  or chili sauce

2 C. chopped red cabbage

2 C. shredded lettuce

1 C. pineapple chunks

16 sugar snap peas,
  sliced lengthwise

½ C. sliced Enoki
  mushrooms

½ C. chopped radishes

Toasted sesame
  seeds, optional*

Cut each chicken breast half, lengthwise, into 4 strips. Thread 2 of the chicken strips on each of eight 6″ wooden skewers. Place in a 2-quart rectangular microwave-safe baking dish and set aside. In a jar with a tight-fitting lid, combine oil, white wine vinegar, sesame seed oil, soy sauce, dry mustard and crushed red pepper. Cover jar and shake well. In a small bowl, stir together 2 tablespoons of the sesame dressing with plum or chili sauce. Brush mixture over the chicken kabobs. Cover dish with waxed paper and microwave on high for 2 minutes. Turn kabobs over, rearrange in dish and brush again with the dressing mixture. Microwave for 2 to 4 minutes or until chicken is no longer pink. Combine red cabbage and lettuce and divide among 4 salad plates. Top lettuce with kabobs, pineapple chunks, sugar snap peas, mushrooms and chopped radishes. Drizzle remaining sesame dressing over salad. If desired, sprinkle with toasted sesame seeds before serving.

*To toast, place sesame seeds in a single layer on a baking sheet. Bake at 350° for 10 minutes or until seeds are golden brown.

Ginger Dill Fish Fillets

⅓ C. mayonnaise
2 T. sour cream
½ tsp. minced dried onion
¼ tsp. ground ginger
¼ tsp. dried dillweed
Dash of salt
¼ C. peeled and cooked or canned small shrimp

1 lb. cod, sole or flounder fillets
1 T. margarine or butter
Lemon wedges, optional
Fresh dill sprigs, optional

In a small bowl, combine mayonnaise, sour cream, minced dried onion, ginger, dillweed and salt. Stir in shrimp and set aside. Place fillets in a 2-quart rectangular microwave-safe baking dish. Dot fillets with margarine. Cover baking dish with waxed paper. Cook in the microwave on high for 4 to 7 minutes or until fish just begins to flake easily, turning dish once. Spoon dressing mixture over fish. Cover and cook in the microwave on high for an additional 1 to 2 minutes or until sauce is heated throughout. Serve with lemon wedges and garnish with fresh dill sprigs, if desired.

Quick Lasagna Casserole

8 oz. dried miniature
  lasagna noodles, broken
12 oz. mild or hot bulk
  Italian sausage
2½ C. red pasta
  sauce, any kind

1 egg, beaten
1 C. cottage cheese
2 T. grated Parmesan or
  Romano cheese
¾ C. shredded
  mozzarella cheese

In a large pan over medium high heat, boil four cups water. Add lasagna noodles to boiling water and cook until pasta is tender. Drain water from cooked noodles and set aside. In a microwave-safe 2-quart square baking dish, crumble sausage. Cover with vented plastic wrap and microwave on high for 4 to 6 minutes or until sausage is brown, stirring once or twice. Drain fat from baking dish. Stir cooked pasta and pasta sauce into sausage in dish. Cover and microwave on high for 2 to 3 minutes or until heated throughout, stirring once. In a medium bowl, mix egg, cottage cheese and Parmesan or Romano cheese. Spoon cheese mixture over pasta mixture. Cover and microwave on high for an additional 6 to 7 minutes or until heated throughout. Sprinkle casserole with mozzarella cheese. Cover and let stand for 5 minutes before serving.

Microwave Cheesy Potato Soup

4 medium baking potatoes
1 medium onion, sliced
2 T. butter
2 T. flour
1 tsp. beef
  bouillon granules
2 C. water
1 (12 oz.) can
  evaporated milk

1 C. shredded
  Cheddar cheese
1 T. fresh chopped parsley
1 tsp. Worcestershire sauce
¾ tsp. pepper
¼ tsp. salt

Scrub potatoes and prick several times with a fork. On a microwave-safe plate, arrange potatoes. Cook potatoes in the microwave on high power, uncovered, for 14 to 17 minutes or until tender, rearranging potatoes once. Peel potatoes and coarsely chop. In a large microwave-safe bowl, combine onion slices and butter. Cover with waxed paper and cook in the microwave on high for 2 minutes or until onion is tender, stirring once. Stir in flour and bouillon granules. Add water and stir until completely combined. Cover with waxed paper and cook in the microwave for an additional 4 to 5 minutes or until mixture is slightly thickened and bubbly, stirring after every minute. Add chopped potatoes, evaporated milk, shredded cheese, chopped parsley, Worcestershire sauce, pepper and salt. Cover and cook in microwave for 3 to 4 minutes or until cheese is melted and soup is heated throughout, stirring once or twice.

Shrimp Casserole

1 lb. medium shrimp, peeled and deveined

1 medium onion, halved lengthwise and sliced

1 T. vegetable oil

⅓ C. brown sugar

3 T. cornstarch

¼ tsp. ground ginger

¼ tsp. pepper

1 (15¼ oz.) can pineapple chunks in juice

¼ C. soy sauce

¼ C. vinegar

1 medium green sweet pepper, cut into strips

1 (8 oz.) can sliced water chestnuts, drained

3 C. hot cooked rice

Rinse shrimp and pat dry with paper towels. In a 2-quart microwave-safe dish, combine onion and vegetable oil. Cover and cook in microwave on high for 2 minutes. Add shrimp to onion in dish, cover and cook on high for 2 to 3 minutes more or until shrimp turn opaque, stirring once. Drain shrimp and onion in a colander. In the same dish, combine brown sugar, cornstarch, ground ginger and pepper. Stir in undrained pineapple, soy sauce and vinegar. Cook in microwave on high, uncovered, for 5 to 6 minutes or until thickened and bubbly, stirring after every minute. Stir in sweet pepper strips. Cook in the microwave on high, uncovered, for 1 minute. Stir in shrimp mixture and water chestnuts. Cook in microwave on high, uncovered, for an additional 30 to 45 seconds or until heated throughout, stirring once. Serve shrimp casserole over hot cooked rice.

Single Shepherd's Pies

1 (7 oz.) pkg. instant
  mashed potatoes
1 (10 oz.) pkg. frozen peas
  and carrots, thawed
1½ C. cubed cooked
  lamb or beef

1 (12 oz.) jar beef gravy
½ tsp. dried basil
1 T. finely shredded
  Cheddar cheese

Preheat oven to 350°. According to directions on package, prepare instant mashed potatoes. In a medium bowl, mix peas and carrots, lamb or beef, beef gravy and basil. Divide mixture evenly among four 12 ounce casseroles dishes. Top lamb or beef and vegetable mixture with prepared mashed potatoes and shredded cheese. Bake, uncovered, for 30 to 35 minutes or until casserole is heated throughout.

"Want to make your
computer go really fast?
Throw it out a window."
~Anonymous~

Fab Fettuccine with Creamy Ham Sauce

1 (12 oz.) can
  evaporated milk
2 tsp. cornstarch
½ tsp. dry mustard
¼ tsp. salt
⅛ tsp. pepper
⅓ C. shredded Swiss cheese
1 C. chopped fully
  cooked ham

1 C. cooked and chopped
  broccoli or cauliflower
1 (2½ oz.) can sliced mushrooms, drained
3 C. cooked fettuccine
2 T. sliced green
  onions, optional

In a medium saucepan over medium heat, cook and stir evaporated milk, cornstarch, dry mustard, salt and pepper until thick and bubbly. Cook and stir for an additional 2 minutes. Add cheese to the mixture and stir until melted. Stir in chopped ham, chopped broccoli or cauliflower and drained mushrooms. Cook and stir until heated throughout. Pour mixture over cooked fettuccine on a serving platter. If desired, garnish with sliced green onions before serving.

Spiced Chicken

1 T. brown sugar
3 T. dry sherry
2 T. soy sauce
1 tsp. minced
   fresh gingerroot
1 tsp. minced garlic
¼ tsp. Chinese
   five-spice powder
4 large chicken
   thighs, skinned

1 tsp. cornstarch
1 T. cold water
1 green onion,
   thinly sliced
2 C. cooked wild and
   white rice, optional
2 C. steamed
   watercress, optional

In a shallow 1½ -quart microwave-safe dish, combine brown sugar, dry sherry, soy sauce, minced gingerroot, garlic and Chinese five-spice powder. Add chicken to mixture and turn to coat. Cover dish and microwave on high for 10 minutes, turning chicken halfway through. Transfer chicken to a platter. In a small bowl, dissolve cornstarch in cold water and stir mixture into remaining juices in microwave dish. Microwave mixture on high, uncovered, for an additional 1½ minutes. Stir and pour over chicken. Garnish with green onions. Serve over a bed of wild and white rice and steamed watercress, if desired.

Manageable Microwave Meatloaf

2 slices bacon,
  cut into ½″ pieces
1 (8 oz.) can tomato
  sauce, divided
½ C. shredded zucchini
⅓ C. uncooked oats
¼ C. finely chopped onion
1 T. minced fresh
  parsley, divided

1 T. water
1 tsp. minced
  garlic, divided
¼ tsp. dried thyme
¾ tsp. salt
¼ tsp. pepper
1 lb. lean ground beef
½ lb. ground turkey

In a microwave-safe dish, place bacon pieces. Cover with paper towel. Microwave bacon on high for 2 minutes or until just crisp and drain. In a large bowl, combine 2 tablespoons tomato sauce, zucchini, oats, onion, 2 teaspoons parsley, water, ½ teaspoon garlic, thyme, salt and pepper. Add ground beef and ground turkey to the mixture. Shape meat into a 4 x 7″ loaf. Place meatloaf in a 2-quart dish with lid. Microwave on high, uncovered, for 5 minutes, turning once. Combine remaining tomato sauce, remaining parsley and remaining garlic. Pour sauce mixture evenly over meatloaf. Cover and cook in the microwave on medium power for 25 minutes, turning once. Top with reserved crisp bacon and microwave, covered, for an additional 10 minutes.

Fast Side Dishes

Green Beans and Almonds

1 (15 oz.) can green
    beans, drained
1 (14 oz.) can stewed
    tomatoes, drained

Italian seasoning to taste
⅓ C. sliced almonds

In a medium saucepan over medium heat, cook the green beans and tomatoes until heated throughout. Season with Italian seasoning. Stir in the sliced almonds just before serving.

Asian-Style Zucchini

1 tsp. butter
1 large zucchini,
  cut into 1″ slices
2 T. soy sauce

2 T. sesame seeds
Garlic powder to taste
Pepper to taste

In a medium skillet over medium heat, melt the butter. Stir in the zucchini slices and cook until lightly browned. Sprinkle with soy sauce and sesame seeds. Season with garlic powder and pepper to taste. Continue cooking until zucchini is well coated and tender.

Parmesan Asparagus

1 T. butter
¼ C. olive oil
1 lb. fresh asparagus
  spears, trimmed

¾ C. grated
  Parmesan cheese
Salt and pepper to taste

In a large skillet over medium heat, combine butter with olive oil, stirring until butter is melted. Add asparagus spears and cook, stirring occasionally, for about 10 minutes, or to desired firmness. Drain off excess oil and sprinkle with grated Parmesan cheese, salt and pepper to taste.

Apricot Acorn Squash

1 acorn squash,
  halved and seeded
Salt to taste

2 tsp. butter, divided
3 T. apricot
  preserves, divided

Preheat oven to 400°. Place squash halves cut-side-down in a 9″ square baking dish. Fill the dish with ¼″ water. Bake for 40 minutes. Remove squash from oven and set the oven to broil. Turn squash cut-side-up in the dish and season lightly with salt to taste. Place 1 teaspoon butter and 1 ½ tablespoons apricot preserves in each squash half. Return to oven and broil for 5 minutes, or until butter is melted and squash is lightly browned.

Bacon
Baked Beans

½ lb. bacon, chopped
1 onion, finely chopped
2 (15 oz.) cans baked beans

¼ C. brown sugar
¼ C. ketchup
¼ C. prepared mustard

In a large deep skillet over medium heat, cook bacon until evenly browned. Add the chopped onion and sauté until tender. Drain excess oil from skillet. Stir in the baked beans, brown sugar, ketchup and mustard. Cook, stirring occasionally, until bubbly and heated throughout.

Brisk Baked Pineapple

1 (8 oz.) can crushed
    pineapple in juice
⅓ C. sugar

½ tsp. ground cinnamon
2 eggs, beaten
1 T. quick-cooking tapioca

Preheat oven to 350°. In a small baking dish, mix the pineapple with juice, sugar, cinnamon, beaten eggs and tapioca. Bake for 30 minutes. Remove from oven and let cool slightly before serving.

"People forget how fast
you did a job — but they
remember how well you did it."
~Howard Newton~

Balsamic Carrots

1 T. olive oil
3 C. baby carrots

1½ T. balsamic vinegar
1 T. brown sugar

In a medium skillet over medium high heat, warm olive oil. Sauté carrots in oil for about 10 minutes, or until tender. Stir in balsamic vinegar and brown sugar, mixing until well coated. Serve immediately.

Candied Acorn Squash

1 acorn squash,
    halved and seeded
¼ C. butter, divided

¼ C. brown
    sugar, divided

Place both halves of the squash cut-side-up on a micro-wave-safe plate or dish. Put 2 tablespoons butter and 2 tablespoons brown sugar into the cavity of each half. Cook for 8 to 10 minutes in the microwave on full power. Rotate the squash a couple of times to ensure even cooking. When the flesh of the acorn squash is soft, scoop out soft flesh and place in a medium bowl. Mash slightly to blend the ingredients and serve.

Creamy Peas

2 C. frozen green
  peas, thawed
⅔ C. water
⅛ tsp. salt
3 T. butter

⅓ C. heavy
  whipping cream
2 T. flour
1 T. sugar

In a medium saucepan over high heat, combine peas, water and salt. Bring to a boil then stir in butter. In a small bowl, whisk together heavy whipping cream, flour and sugar. Stir mixture into peas. Cook over medium-high heat until thick and bubbly, about 5 minutes.

Lovely Lemon Pepper Pasta

1 lb. uncooked
   spaghetti pasta
2 T. olive oil

3 T. lemon juice
1 T. dried basil
Pepper to taste

In a large pot over high heat, bring 6 cups water to a boil. Add spaghetti pasta to boiling water and cook until pasta is tender. Drain water from spaghetti and set aside. In a small bowl, combine olive oil, lemon juice, dried basil and pepper. Mix well and toss with the pasta. Transfer pasta to a serving bowl. Serve hot or cold.

Sunflower Seed and Apple Salad

2 green apples, washed, cored and cubed

½ C. sunflower seeds

1 head Romaine lettuce, rinsed and chopped

2 dill pickles, diced

2 tomatoes, diced

½ C. ranch dressing

In a large bowl, mix together cubed apples, sunflower seeds, chopped lettuce, diced pickles and diced tomatoes. Pour ranch dressing over ingredients and toss to coat.

Snappy
Fruit Salad

2 C. sliced
   fresh strawberries
1 lb. seedless green
   grapes, halved

3 bananas, peeled
   and sliced
1 (8 oz.) container
   strawberry yogurt

In a large bowl, toss together sliced strawberries, halved grapes, sliced bananas and strawberry yogurt. Mix well and serve immediately.

"The fastest way to succeed is to look as if you're playing by somebody else's rules, while quietly playing by your own."
~Michael Konda~

Balsamic
Bow Tie Pasta

1 (16 oz.) pkg. bowtie pasta
2 green onions, chopped
1 (6 oz.) pkg. crumbled
  feta cheese

½ C. balsamic vinegar
¼ C. olive oil
2 C. chopped tomatoes

In a large pot, bring 6 cups of lightly salted water to a boil. Add bowtie pasta and cook for 8 to 10 minutes until al dente. Drain pasta and place in ice water until cool. Remove cooked pasta from water and transfer to a serving bowl. Toss together pasta, chopped green onion, feta cheese, balsamic vinegar, olive oil and chopped tomato. Chill in the refrigerator for 1 to 2 hours before serving.

Fast Appetizers

Piping Hot Ponderosas

1 C. butter
5½ T. minced garlic
2½ T. crumbled
  bleu cheese
3½ T. herbs de Provence
1 T. crushed red
  pepper flakes

Salt and pepper to taste
Dash of Worcestershire
  sauce
1 thin baguette, cut into
  thick slices

Preheat the grill to high heat. In a medium saucepan over medium heat, melt butter. Mix in minced garlic, bleu cheese, herbs de Provence, red pepper flakes, salt, pepper and Worcestershire sauce. Dunk each baguette slice in the butter mixture to thoroughly coat. Place coated baguette slices in a bowl and toss with any remaining butter mixture. Place the baguette slices on the prepared grill and toast for 1 minute on each side, or to desired crispness.

Bacon Blanket Water Chestnuts

½ lb. bacon, cut in half
1 (8 oz.) can water
  chestnuts, drained

¾ C. ketchup
½ C. brown sugar

Preheat oven to 375°. Wrap ½ strip of bacon around each water chestnut. In a small bowl, combine ketchup and brown sugar. Dip each wrapped water chestnut into ketchup mixture. Place wrapped water chestnuts in a lightly greased 9 x 13″ baking dish. Bake, covered, for 20 minutes, or until bacon is crisp.

"Good, fast, cheap:
choose any two."
~Anonymous~

Caramel Banana Fluff

2 bananas,
  peeled and sliced
1 T. vanilla
2 T. butter, melted

1 (8 oz.) can refrigerated
  crescent rolls
1 C. caramel topping

Preheat oven to 350°. In a small bowl, combine sliced bananas, vanilla and melted butter. Toss to coat. On a baking sheet, unroll crescent rolls, leaving every two triangles attached to form 4 squares. Place ¼ of the banana mixture in the center of each square. Bake for 11 to 13 minutes, or until pastry is golden brown. Heat caramel topping and drizzle over banana mixture. Serve warm.

Cup of Cheese Cake

16 vanilla wafer cookies
2 (8 oz.) pkgs. cream
cheese, softened

¾ C. sugar
2 eggs
1 tsp. vanilla

Preheat oven to 350°. Line muffin pans with paper liners. Place 1 vanilla wafer cookie in the bottom of each paper liner. In a medium bowl, blend together cream cheese and sugar. In a separate bowl, beat eggs and vanilla until smooth. Add egg mixture to cream cheese mixture and blend until smooth. Pour mixture over wafers in each liner. Bake for 15 minutes, until golden and set.

Chocolate Éclair

2 pkgs. of 8 graham
  crackers, divided
2 (3 oz.) pkgs. instant
  vanilla pudding mix
3 C. milk

1 (8 oz.) container frozen
  whipped topping, thawed
1 (16 oz.) pkg. prepared
  chocolate frosting

Line the bottom of a 9 x 13″ dish with ⅓ of the graham crackers. In a large bowl, combine vanilla pudding mix and milk. Stir briskly, using a wire whisk. Fold in whipped topping. Spread half of the pudding mixture over the graham cracker layer in dish. Top with another layer of graham crackers and the remaining pudding mixture. Top with a final layer of graham crackers. Carefully frost graham crackers with chocolate frosting. Refrigerate until ready to serve.

Dessert Crepes

4 eggs, lightly beaten
1⅓ C. milk
2 T. butter, melted

1 C. flour
2 T. sugar
½ tsp. salt

In large bowl, whisk together eggs, milk, melted butter, flour, sugar and salt, stirring until smooth. Place a medium skillet over medium heat. Grease skillet with a small amount of butter or oil applied with a brush or paper towel. Using a serving spoon or small ladle, spoon about 3 tablespoons of the crepe batter into the hot skillet, tilting the pan to cover the bottom surface of the pan. Cook over medium heat for 1 to 2 minutes on each side, or until golden brown. Serve immediately.

Cheap

Ranch Chicken Casserole

1 (3 lb.) whole chicken
1 (10¾ oz.) can cream
  of mushroom soup
1 (10¾ oz.) can cream
  of chicken soup
1 (10 oz.) can diced
  tomatoes, drained
1 green chili pepper, diced

½ (10¾ oz.) can
  chicken broth
12 corn tortillas,
  cut into pieces
1 onion, chopped
2 C. shredded
  Cheddar cheese

Preheat oven to 350°. In a medium saucepan over medium high heat, cook whole chicken. Fill saucepan with a little lightly salted water and heat until chicken is tender. Remove bones from chicken and cut chicken meat into pieces. In a medium bowl, mix cream of mushroom soup, cream of chicken soup, diced tomatoes, green chili pepper and chicken broth until smooth and set aside. Into a greased 8″ square dish, place a layer of ½ the chicken pieces, ½ the tortilla pieces, ½ the onion, ½ the cheese and ½ the soup mixture. Repeat the layers and top with the remaining shredded cheese. Bake, uncovered, for 1 hour.

Three Bean Casserole

½ lb. bacon, chopped
1 lb. ground beef
5 C. kidney beans
5 C. lima beans
5 C. prepared pork
  and beans

1 large onion, chopped
½ C. brown sugar
½ C. ketchup

Preheat oven to 350°. In a medium skillet over medium high heat, brown chopped bacon and ground beef. In an 8″ square dish, mix cooked bacon, ground beef, kidney beans, lima beans, pork and beans, chopped onion, brown sugar and ketchup. Mix until well combined. Bake for 35 minutes.

"That man is the richest
whose pleasures are
the cheapest."
~Henry David Thoreau~

Gee Whiz Cheesy Chicken Casserole

1 (8 oz.) jar Cheese Whiz
½ C. milk
7 oz. spaghetti, broken in thirds, cooked and drained
2 T. butter
1¼ C. cooked chopped broccoli
1 C. cooked chopped chicken
1 (4 oz.) can mushrooms, drained
2 T. chopped pimento
¼ tsp. salt
¼ tsp. dried sage

Preheat oven to 350°. In a medium bowl, mix Cheese Whiz and milk. In a separate bowl, toss cooked spaghetti with butter. In a large bowl, combine cheese mixture, spaghetti, cooked broccoli, chopped chicken, drained mushrooms, chopped pimento, salt and dried sage. Spoon mixture into an 8″ square dish. Cover dish and bake for 30 to 35 minutes. Stir well before serving.

Budget Beef Stroganoff

4 T. butter, divided
½ C. diced onions
Garlic powder to taste
2 T. flour
2 T. salt
¼ tsp. pepper
1 lb. ground beef
1 (4 oz.) can sliced
  mushrooms, drained

1 (15½ oz.) can
  beef consommé
1 T. vinegar
1 (6 oz.) can tomato paste
1 (12 oz.) pkg. uncooked
  egg noodles
2 C. sour cream

In a large skillet over medium heat, melt 2 tablespoons butter. Add diced onions and garlic to taste and sauté until soft. In a medium bowl, combine flour, salt, pepper and ground beef. Add ground beef and sliced mushrooms to skillet with onions and cook, stirring often, for 6 minutes. Stir in beef consommé, vinegar and tomato paste. Let the beef simmer, uncovered, for 10 minutes. Stir often and cook to desired consistency. In a medium pot, cook egg noodles according to package directions. Drain noodles and rinse under hot water. In the same pot, melt remaining 2 tablespoons butter. Return egg noodles to pot. Blend sour cream into beef mixture just before serving and simmer for 2 minutes, or until heated throughout. Serve beef mixture over noodles.

Cheap and Easy Chicken

1 (8 oz.) carton
  plain yogurt
1 to 3 cloves garlic, minced
1 tsp. salt
½ tsp. cardamom powder

½ tsp. chili powder
¼ tsp. ground cinnamon
¼ tsp. ground ginger
4 boneless, skinless
  chicken breasts

Preheat broiler. In an 8″ square dish, mix plain yogurt, minced garlic, salt, cardamom powder, chili powder, ground cinnamon and ground ginger. Pour half the marinade in a small bowl and set aside to reserve for later use. Add chicken to the remaining marinade mixture and turn to coat. Chill chicken and marinade in refrigerator for at least 2 hours. Remove chicken from marinade and place skin-side-up on broiler rack. Broil until chicken is seared on top. Turn chicken over and broil for an additional 2 to 3 minutes or less. Remove chicken and place on serving platter. In a medium pan, simmer reserved marinade for 5 minutes. Pour simmering sauce over chicken before serving.

Easy Oriental Dinner

1 lb. ground turkey
1 (1 lb.) pkg. frozen
  mixed vegetables

4 (3 oz.) pkgs.
  ramen noodles
1 T. vegetable oil

In a medium skillet over medium heat, brown ground turkey. According to directions on package, cook mixed vegetables and drain well. According to directions on package, cook ramen noodles, however, do not add seasoning packets. Drain water from noodles. Add vegetable oil to noodles and mix. Add 2 of the seasoning packets to noodles and mix well. Add remaining 2 seasoning packets to browned meat and mix well. Add vegetables and noodles to meat. Mix well before serving.

Spicy
Baked Fish

1 lb. cod fillets
¼ T. paprika
¼ tsp. garlic powder
¼ tsp. onion powder
⅛ tsp. pepper

⅛ tsp. dried oregano
⅛ tsp. dried thyme
1 T. lemon juice
1½ T. margarine, melted

Preheat oven to 350°. Separate fish into four fillets or pieces. In an ungreased 9 x 13″ dish, place fish. In a small bowl, combine paprika, garlic powder, onion powder, pepper, dried oregano and dried thyme. Sprinkle seasoning mixture and lemon juice evenly over fish. Drizzle margarine evenly over fish. Bake until fish flakes easily with a fork, about 20 to 25 minutes. Remove from oven and transfer fish to individual serving plates.

Chicken and Vegetables

1½ T. margarine
1 tsp. garlic powder
1 onion, chopped
1 lb. boneless,
  skinless chicken thighs,
  cut into strips

1 (10 oz.) pkg. frozen
  cut green beans
¼ tsp. pepper

In a medium skillet over medium heat, melt margarine. Add garlic powder and chopped onions to margarine and stir until blended. Cook until chopped onions are tender, about 5 minutes. Remove from skillet. Place chicken in the skillet. Cook over medium heat, until chicken is thoroughly done and no longer pink in color, about 12 minutes. Remove chicken from skillet and keep warm. In the same skillet over medium low heat, cover and cook frozen green beans, pepper and cooked onions for about 5 minutes. Add cooked chicken to vegetable mixture. Continue cooking, stirring occasionally, until heated throughout, about 3 minutes.

Simple Tator Tot Casserole

2 lbs. ground beef
1 (10¾ oz.) can cream of
  mushroom soup
1 (2 lb.) bag frozen
  tater tots

1 C. shredded
  Cheddar cheese

Preheat oven to 350°. In a medium skillet over medium high heat, brown ground beef. Drain beef and place in the bottom of a greased 9 x 13″ dish. Mix cream of mushroom soup with cooked ground beef and sprinkle with shredded Cheddar cheese. Top with frozen tater tots. Bake, covered, for 45 minutes. Uncover and bake for an additional 15 minutes. Remove from oven and serve.

"We'd all like a reputation
for generosity, and we'd
all like to buy it cheap."
~Mignon McLaughlin~

BBQ Beef Cups

1 lb ground beef
½ C. barbecue sauce
1 T. minced
  onion, optional
1 T. brown sugar

1 (8 oz.) can
  refrigerated biscuits
¾ C. shredded
  Cheddar cheese

Preheat oven to 400°. In a medium skillet over medium heat, brown ground beef and drain. Add barbecue sauce, minced onion and brown sugar to cooked ground beef. In a greased muffin pan, press each biscuit into the bottoms and sides of each muffin cup. Spoon an even amount of beef mixture into each biscuit cup and top with shredded Cheddar cheese. Bake for 10 to 12 minutes. Remove BBQ Beef Cups from muffin pan and serve.

Classic Corn Dogs

4 C. frying oil
1 C. flour
1½ tsp. baking powder
½ tsp. salt
2 tsp. cornmeal
3 T. shortening

1 large egg
¾ C. milk
1 (16 oz.) pkg.
  beef hot dogs
10 wooden skewers

In an electric deep fat fryer, warm frying oil. In a medium bowl, mix flour, baking powder, salt, cornmeal, shortening, egg and milk. Insert a wooden skewer into one end of each hot dog. Dip each hot dog into the batter. Remove from batter and immediately dip coated hot dogs in hot oil. Fry corn dogs until brown. Remove from fryer and drain corn dogs on paper towels. Let corn dogs cool before serving.

Bacon Potato Soup

1 lb. potatoes,
  peeled and cubed
3 qts. water
1 tsp. vegetable oil
1 onion, chopped
½ C. chopped
  bacon, uncooked

2 T. flour
2 tsp. beef
  bouillon granules
2 T. chopped fresh parsley
2 T. chopped fresh chives
Salt and pepper to taste

In a large pot over medium heat, boil cubed potatoes in 3 quarts of water. Do not drain water from pot. In a skillet over medium heat, warm vegetable oil. Add chopped onion and chopped bacon to vegetable oil. Sauté until the onion is golden brown. Add flour to bacon and onion mixture, stirring until browned. Transfer onion and bacon mixture to the pot with cubed potatoes and water. Stir until soup boils and thickens. Add beef bouillon granules, chopped fresh parsley, chopped fresh chives, salt and pepper.

Crock Pot
Tuna Casserole

1 (6½ oz.) can tuna
  in water, drained
1 (10¾ oz.) can cream
  of mushroom soup

1 (16 oz.) pkg. shell
  pasta, uncooked
2 C. water
Salt and pepper to taste

In a medium crockpot, combine drained tuna, cream of mushroom soup, uncooked pasta, water and salt and pepper. Cover and cook on low setting until noodles are soft, about 4 hours. Remove mixture from crockpot and let cool for about 3 minutes before serving.

Pumpkin Nut Soup

1 (4½ lb.) peeled and
   roughly chopped
   pumpkin
10 C. water
2 onions, roughly chopped
2 potatoes,
   roughly chopped

2 T. chicken
   bouillon granules
2 T. powdered milk
2 T. creamy peanut butter
Salt and pepper to taste

In a large pot over medium high heat, bring chopped pumpkin, water, chopped onion and chopped potatoes to a boil for 20 minutes. Add chicken bouillon granules, powdered milk, creamy peanut butter, salt and pepper. Using an electric mixer, blend mixture until soup is smooth, or reaches desired consistency.

"If you want to say it with flowers,
a single rose says: 'I'm cheap!'"
~Delta Burke~

French Onion Soup

6 large onions, chopped
2 tsp. butter
2 cloves garlic, chopped
Pinch of sugar
½ tsp. dry mustard
Nutmeg to taste

2 T. flour
3 liters water
3 tsp. beef
  bouillon granules
Salt and pepper to taste

In a large pot over medium high heat, cook chopped onions, butter, chopped garlic, sugar, dry mustard and nutmeg until onions are golden in color. Add flour to pot and stir into onion mixture. Cook for 2 minutes. Slowly add the water, then beef bouillon granules, salt and pepper. Bring soup to a boil for 15 minutes, stirring often.

Apple Yam Casserole

1¼ 1b. yams
½ C. water
1 lb. apples, peeled
   and cut into ½″ slices
1 C. apple juice

2 T. cornstarch
3 T. water
½ C. honey
⅓ C. wheat germ

Preheat oven to 350°. In a large pot with a tight-fitting lid over medium high heat, steam yams in water for 15 to 20 minutes, or until tender. Peel and slice yams into ½″ thick pieces. In an 8″ square dish, layer yams on the bottom. Lay apple slices on top of yams in dish. In a small pan over medium high heat, bring apple juice to a boil. Add cornstarch and water to juice. Cook until sauce is clear and thickened. Add honey to sauce. Spoon sauce over apples and sprinkle with wheat germ. Bake until apples are tender, about 30 minutes to 1 hour.

Chili Cheese Cornbread

2 (15½ oz.) cans
  chili with beans
2 C. shredded
  Cheddar cheese

⅓ C. milk
1 egg
1 (8 oz.) box cornbread mix

Preheat oven to 375°. In a greased 8 x 11″ dish, spread chili with beans evenly across bottom. Sprinkle shredded Cheddar cheese over chili. In a medium bowl, combine milk, egg and cornbread mix. Mix well and spread over top of Cheddar cheese. Bake for 15 to 20 minutes, or until cornbread topping is golden brown and thoroughly cooked.

Simple
Macaroni Salad

1 (1 lb.) box elbow
   macaroni, uncooked
4 stalks celery, chopped
3 green onions, chopped

1 green pepper, chopped
½ C. sweet relish
2 C. mayonnaise
Salt and pepper to taste

In a large pan over medium high heat, bring 4 cups water to a boil. Add elbow macaroni to boiling water and cook until pasta is tender. Drain water from pasta and set aside. In a large bowl, mix chopped celery, chopped green onions, chopped green pepper, sweet relish, mayonnaise and cooked macaroni. Toss salad to coat thoroughly. Add salt and pepper to taste.

Baked Mac and Cheese

1 (8 oz.) box small shell
   pasta, uncooked
2 C. shredded
   Cheddar cheese
2 large eggs, slightly beaten

¼ tsp. salt
Worcestershire
   sauce to taste
2 C. milk

Preheat oven to 350°. In a large pan over medium high heat, bring 2 quarts water to a boil. Add shell pasta to boiling water and cook until pasta is tender. Drain water from pasta and set aside. In a medium bowl, beat together eggs, salt and Worcestershire sauce. Add milk to egg mixture and mix thoroughly. In a 9″ square dish, place a layer of cooked shell pasta evenly across the bottom and sprinkle Cheddar cheese over top. Pour egg mixture over pasta and cheese. Bake for 45 to 50 minutes, or until set and lightly browned on top.

Nutmeg Potatoes

2 lbs. potatoes, peeled and chopped

2 tsp. butter

3 T. milk

Nutmeg to taste

Salt and pepper to taste

In a large pot over medium heat, cook chopped potatoes in 3 quarts boiling water until tender. In a medium bowl, mash together drained potatoes, butter and milk. Sprinkle nutmeg, salt and pepper to taste over the potatoes. Mash until well combined.

Mashed Potatoes and Onions

2 lbs. potatoes,
   peeled and chopped
2 tsp. butter

3 T. milk
2 onions, finely sliced
Salt and pepper to taste

In a large pot over medium heat, boil chopped potatoes in 3 quarts boiling water until tender. In a medium bowl, mash together drained potatoes, butter and milk. Add sliced onions, salt and pepper to potatoes. Mash until well combined.

Corn Chip Salad

1 T. lime juice
1 T. fish sauce
½ T. vegetable oil
½ T. mild sweet chili sauce
1 small head
  lettuce, shredded
½ cucumber, diced
½ red pepper, diced

2½ C. drained
  pineapple chunks
1 onion, finely sliced
1 C. baby corn spears
1 C. diced cooked chicken
2 avocados, peeled
  and diced
1 (8 oz.) bag corn chips

In a jar with a tight-fitting lid, combine lime juice, fish sauce, vegetable oil and chili sauce. Cover tightly and shake jar to mix dressing. Set aside. In a large bowl, combine shredded lettuce, diced cucumber, diced red pepper, pineapple chunks, onion slices and baby corn spears. Add cooked chicken and dried avocados to salad and pour half of the dressing over top. Toss lightly to combine. Place a layer of corn chips on 4 separate salad plates and top each with some of the salad. Drizzle remaining dressing over each salad before serving.

Sweet Citrus Salad

1 Granny Smith
  apple, thinly sliced
1 T. lemon juice
2 celery stalks, chopped
1 small red onion,
  sliced into rings
1 (1 lb.) can pineapple
  chunks, drained

2 C. sliced cherry tomatoes
1 (11 oz.) can mandarin
  oranges, drained
1 small head
  lettuce, shredded
½ C. cashews
¼ C. vinaigrette

In a large bowl, toss apple slices in lemon juice. Add chopped celery, sliced red onion, pineapple chunks, sliced cherry tomatoes, drained mandarin oranges and shredded lettuce to Granny Smith apples. Toss salad to combine. Chill in the refrigerator for 30 minutes to 1 hour. Before serving, sprinkle with cashews and pour vinaigrette over salad.

Fruity Cole Slaw

2 C. finely
  shredded cabbage
2 carrots, grated

1 red apple, finely chopped
1 C. mayonnaise

In a medium bowl, combine shredded cabbage, grated carrots, chopped apple and mayonnaise. Toss well to coat. Let cole slaw chill in refrigerator for 30 minutes to 1 hour before serving.

"People say I am cheap,
and I don't mind if they do"
~Ingvar Kamprad~

Tofu Taco Dip

1 (8 oz.) pkg. cream cheese	2 tomatoes, chopped
1 (6 oz.) pkg. soft tofu	2 C. shredded
½ (1 oz.) pkg.	Cheddar cheese
taco seasoning	2 onions, finely chopped
1 green pepper, chopped	1 (8 oz.) bag corn chips

Using an electric mixer, in a medium bowl, beat cream cheese until soft. Add tofu to cream cheese and beat until smooth. Add taco seasoning, chopped green pepper, chopped tomatoes, shredded Cheddar Cheese and chopped onions to cream cheese and tofu mixture. Mix ingredients thoroughly. Serve with corn chips for dipping.

Asparagus Wraps

½ C. crumbled bleu cheese
1 tsp. Worcestershire sauce
1 egg, beaten
1 (8 oz.) pkg. cream
  cheese, softened
Garlic powder to taste

Pepper to taste
1 (14½ oz.) can
  asparagus spears
1 loaf sliced bread
¼ C. butter, melted

Preheat oven to 350°. In a medium bowl, using an electric mixer, mix crumbled bleu cheese, Worcestershire sauce, beaten egg, cream cheese, garlic powder and pepper. Spread some of the cream cheese mixture on each slice of bread. Place 1 asparagus spear over cream cheese mixture on each slice of bread and roll up. Roll the asparagus wraps in melted butter and cut each wrap into thirds. Arrange wraps on an ungreased baking sheet and bake for 20 minutes.

Bacon Onion Wheels

⅓ C. butter, softened
¾ C. finely chopped onion
8 slices bacon, cooked
and crumbled

3 T. fresh chopped parsley
2 (8 oz.) cans refrigerated
crescent rolls

Preheat oven to 375°. In a medium bowl, combine butter, chopped onion, crumbled bacon and chopped parsley. On a greased baking sheet, unroll crescent rolls and separate into 8 rectangles. Firmly press perforations on crescent rolls to seal so rectangles do not tear apart. Spread butter mixture evenly over dough. Roll up each rectangle, beginning with short side and pinch seam to seal. Cut each roll into 4 slices. Bake for 15 minutes, or until golden.

Broiled Cheesy Potato Skins

4 large potatoes
2 tsp. margarine
Salt to taste
1 C. shredded Monterey
  Jack cheese

4 slices bacon, cooked
  and crumbled

Preheat oven to 425°. Prick potatoes with a fork to allow steam to escape. Place potatoes directly on oven rack and bake potatoes until tender, about 1 hour. Remove from oven and allow potatoes to cool slightly. Cut each potato lengthwise into halves. Scoop out fresh from potatoes, leaving a ⅜″ shell. Spread inside of shells with margarine and sprinkle with salt to taste. Cut each potato into 6 pieces and sprinkle with shredded cheese and crumbled bacon. Place potato pieces on a baking sheet. Change oven setting to broil. Broil potato pieces about 5″ from heat until cheese is melted, about 2 minutes.

Cheap Desserts

Microwave Peanut Brittle

1 C. sugar	1 tsp. butter
½ C. corn syrup	1 tsp. vanilla
1½ C. peanuts	1 tsp. baking soda

Spray a baking sheet with nonstick vegetable spray. In a medium microwave-safe bowl, combine sugar and corn syrup. Microwave on high power for 4 minutes. Stir in peanuts. Microwave on high for an additional 4 minutes. Stir in butter and vanilla. Return to microwave for 2 minutes. Stir in baking soda until light and foamy. Pour peanut brittle onto prepared baking sheet and spread evenly with a spatula. Let peanut brittle cool. Break into pieces before serving.

Peppermint Kisses

2 large egg whites
⅛ tsp. salt
⅛ tsp. cream of tartar

½ C. sugar
2 peppermint candies, crushed

Preheat oven to 225°. Arrange oven racks to divide oven in thirds. Line two baking sheets with foil. In a large bowl, using an electric mixer, beat egg whites, salt and cream of tartar until soft peaks form. Gradually add sugar and beat at medium speed for 5 to 6 minutes. Drop mixture by teaspoonfuls onto baking sheets. Sprinkle each with crushed peppermint candies. Bake for 1½ hours, or until peppermint kisses look dry and white.

"Always laugh when you can.
It is cheap medicine."
Lord Byron

Strawberry Rice Pudding

1 (10 oz.) pkg. frozen sliced
    strawberries, thawed
3½ C. milk
½ C. long grain rice

4 tsp. sugar
1¼ C. vanilla
    frozen yogurt

Remove strawberries from freezer and let thaw. Meanwhile, in a medium saucepan over medium heat, bring milk, rice and sugar to a boil. Reduce heat to low, cover, and cook for 50 to 55 minutes, stirring occasionally, until rice is tender. Pour mixture into a medium bowl and chill in refrigerator for 1 hour. Drain strawberries. In a blender, process strawberries at medium speed until smooth. Pour pureed strawberries into a small bowl. Soften frozen yogurt in refrigerator. Stir 2 tablespoons frozen yogurt into strawberries. Stir remaining yogurt into rice mixture. Spoon strawberry mixture into dessert glasses and top with rice pudding mixture.

Chocolate Crisps

2 C. chocolate chips   1 (10 oz.) pkg. Milk Duds
¼ C. margarine   1 T. water
5 C. crispy rice cereal

In a large microwave-safe bowl, combine chocolate chips and margarine. Cover and microwave on high until chocolate is melted, about 2 minutes. Stir until well blended. Stir in crispy rice cereal, mixing until well coated. In a separate microwave-safe bowl, combine Milk Duds and water. Cover and microwave on high for 1 minute or mixture is pourable. Stir into cereal mixture. Spread mixture into a 9 x 13″ dish. Cover and refrigerate for 30 minutes, or until firm. Cut into bars before serving.

Berry Berry Parfaits

1 (1 oz.) pkg.
  strawberry gelatin
1 C. boiling water
1 C. cold water
2 C. blueberries, divided

2 C. sliced
  strawberries, divided
1¾ C. cold milk
1 (1 oz.) pkg. instant
  vanilla pudding

In a medium bowl, dissolve strawberry gelatin in boiling water. Stir in cold water. Pour into 8 parfait glasses and chill in refrigerator until firm, about 1 hour. Top gelatin with half of the blueberries and half of the sliced strawberries. In a medium bowl, whisk together milk and vanilla pudding mix for 2 minutes, or until slightly thickened. Pour pudding evenly over blueberries and sliced strawberries. Top with remaining blueberries and remaining sliced strawberries. Cover and refrigerate for 1 additional hour.

Minute Cookies

½ C. butter
½ C. milk
2 C. sugar

3 C. quick-cooking oats
5 T. cocoa powder
½ C. raisins

In a large saucepan over medium high heat, place butter, milk and sugar. Bring mixture to a boil, stirring occasionally. Boil for 1 minute. Remove from heat. Stir in quick-cooking oats, cocoa powder and raisins. Drop by tablespoonfuls onto waxed paper. Let cool before serving.

"Don't marry for money; you can borrow it cheaper."
~Scottish Proverb~

Blender Chocolate Mousse

1 (12 oz.) pkg. chocolate
  chips
½ C. sugar

3 eggs
1 C. hot milk
3 T. brandy

In a blender, combine chocolate chips, sugar and eggs. Blend until smooth and add hot milk and brandy. Blend again and pour mixture into 8 small serving cups and refrigerate at least 1 hour.

Warning
Eating raw eggs is not recommended for pregnant women, the elderly and the sick because there is a risk that eggs may be contaminated with salmonella bacteria.

"You'd be surprised
how much it costs
to look this cheap."
~Dolly Parton~

Basic Chicken Parmesan

¼ C. butter, melted
½ tsp. garlic powder
1 T. Dijon mustard
1 tsp. Worcestershire sauce
⅓ C. bread crumbs

⅓ C. grated
   Parmesan cheese
⅛ C. dried parsley
4 boneless, skinless
   chicken breasts

Preheat oven to 350°. In a baking dish, mix together the melted butter, garlic powder, Dijon mustard and Worcestershire sauce. In a medium bowl, combine bread crumbs, grated Parmesan cheese and dried parsley. Dip the chicken breasts in the butter mixture, then in bread crumbs. In a greased 9″ square dish, lay the chicken flat. Bake for 50 to 60 minutes, or until the chicken is no longer pink in the middle.

Laid Back Lemon Garlic Chicken

6 chicken thighs
2 T. vegetable oil
¼ C. lemon juice
½ tsp. dried oregano

¼ tsp. pepper
½ tsp. garlic powder
½ tsp. salt
¼ C. soy sauce

Preheat oven to 400°. In a large bowl, soak the chicken thighs in salted water for 20 minutes. Pat the chicken thighs dry with paper towels and lay flat in a 9″ square baking dish. In a separate bowl, mix vegetable oil, lemon juice, oregano, pepper, garlic powder, salt and soy sauce. Pour the spice mixture over the chicken and let stand for 20 minutes. Bake for 45 minutes, or until the chicken is no longer pink in the middle.

"Almost everything in life is easier to get into than out of."
~Anonymous~

Baked Chicken Breasts with Worcestershire

4 bone-in chicken breasts
1 T. olive oil
Garlic powder to taste

Salt and pepper to taste
¼ C. Worcestershire sauce

Preheat oven to 375°. Rub a small amount of olive oil on each chicken breast. Sprinkle the chicken breasts with garlic powder, salt and pepper. In a 9″ square baking dish, place chicken breasts skin-side-up. Pour Worcestershire sauce over the chicken breasts. Cover the dish tightly with foil and bake for 45 minutes. Remove the foil and bake an additional 15 minutes, or until chicken is no longer pink in the middle.

Italian-Style Baked Eggs

1 small zucchini,
  thinly sliced
½ C. chopped red onion
½ C. chopped red or
  green sweet pepper
2 cloves garlic, minced
2 tsp. olive oil or
  cooking oil

6 egg whites
1 egg
1 C. milk
1 T. chopped fresh basil
¼ C. shredded
  mozzarella cheese
Chopped tomato, optional

Preheat oven to 350°. In a medium skillet over medium high heat, cook zucchini, onion, sweet pepper and garlic in hot oil until onion is tender. Set aside. In a medium bowl, whisk together the egg whites, egg, milk and basil. Stir in zucchini mixture. Pour mixture into 4 individual quiche dishes or shallow casseroles, about 4½″ in diameter. Bake for 15 to 20 minutes or until eggs are set. Sprinkle each serving with mozzarella cheese. Let stand for 5 minutes before serving. If desired, sprinkle with chopped tomato.

Parmesan-Crusted Chicken

2 large eggs
1 T. Dijon
   mustard, optional
2¼ C. finely grated
   Parmesan cheese, divided
1 C. bread crumbs

½ tsp. kosher salt
¼ tsp. pepper
1½ lbs. chicken cutlets
6 T. olive oil, divided
1 head lettuce, torn
1 lemon, cut into wedges

In a shallow bowl, whisk together the eggs and mustard. In a separate bowl, combine 2 cups of the Parmesan cheese, bread crumbs, salt and pepper. Rinse chicken cutlets and pat dry with paper towels. Dip one of the cutlets into the egg mixture, allowing any excess to drip off, then turn to coat in bread crumb mixture. Transfer to a plate. Repeat with the remaining chicken, batter and bread crumb mixture. Heat 2 tablespoons oil in a nonstick skillet over medium high heat. Add half of the cutlets. Cook, turning once, until browned and heated throughout, about 3 to 5 minutes per side. Transfer to a plate. Carefully wipe out the skillet, add 2 more tablespoons oil, and repeat with the remaining cutlets. Divide the cutlets and torn lettuce among individual plates. Drizzle the lettuce with the remaining oil and sprinkle with the remaining Parmesan. Serve with lemon wedges on the side.

Sweet Pea Mint Soup

4 C. frozen peas,
  thawed slightly
¾ C. fresh mint leaves
4 scallions,
  roughly chopped

3 C. chicken or
  vegetable broth
1 tsp. salt
1 tsp. sugar

In a blender, combine peas, mint leaves, chopped scallions, chicken or vegetable broth, salt and sugar. Puree until smooth, at least 1 minute. Pour into individual bowls and serve.

American-Style Chop Suey

1 (16 oz.) pkg. uncooked
   elbow macaroni
1 lb. ground beef
1 onion, chopped

2 (10¾ oz.) cans
   tomato soup
Salt and pepper to taste

In a large pan over medium high heat, boil 6 cups water. Add uncooked macaroni to boiling water and cook until pasta is tender. Drain water from pasta and set aside. In a large skillet over medium high heat, sauté ground beef and the onion for 5 to 10 minutes, or until meat is browned and crumbly. Drain skillet thoroughly and leave meat and onion in the skillet. Add the tomato soup and stir well to combine. Add cooked macaroni to ground beef mixture and mix well. Season with salt and pepper to taste before serving.

Curry Apple Turkey Pita

2 T. olive oil
1 C. sliced onion
2 T. lemon juice
½ lb. cooked turkey,
  cut into chunks
1 T. curry powder,
  or to taste

1 medium apple,
  cored and thinly sliced
3 pita bread rounds
½ C. plain yogurt

In a medium skillet over medium high heat, warm oil. Stir in onion slices and lemon juice. Cook until onion is tender. Mix in turkey and curry powder and continue cooking until heated throughout. Remove skillet from heat and stir in apple slices. Cut pitas in half. Stuff each pita half with the mixture and drizzle with yogurt to serve.

BLAT

8 slices bacon
4 (10″) flour tortillas
4 T. ranch dressing
1 avocado, peeled,
    pitted and diced

1 tomato, chopped
1 C. shredded lettuce

In a deep skillet over medium heat, cook bacon for 10 to 15 minutes, or until crisp. Drain bacon, crumble and set aside. In the microwave, warm tortillas for 30 to 45 seconds each, or until soft. Spread 1 tablespoon ranch dressing down the center of each tortilla. Layer crumbled bacon, diced avocado, chopped tomato and shredded lettuce over the dressing. Roll each tortilla and serve.

Baked Bean Sandwiches

4 English muffins, split
1 (16 oz.) baked beans
1 medium onion,
   thinly sliced

2 medium tomatoes,
   cut into ¼″ slices
4 slices Cheddar cheese
4 slices bacon

Preheat oven to 350°. Arrange English muffin halves on a baking sheet. Place an equal amount of baked beans on each muffin half. Layer beans with onion slices, tomato slices, cheese and bacon slices. Bake muffins for 20 minutes. Set oven to broil and continue cooking for 1 to 2 minutes, until bacon is crisp. Watch constantly during broiling to make sure bacon does not burn. Serve immediately.

Barbecue Chicken Pizza

1 (12″) pre-baked
   pizza crust
½ C. barbecue sauce
½ C. diced grilled chicken
¼ C. chopped
   red bell pepper

¼ C. chopped
   green bell pepper
¼ C. chopped red onion
1 C. shredded Monterey
   Jack cheese

Preheat oven to 450°. Place pizza crust on a baking sheet. Spread pizza crust with barbecue sauce. Scatter diced chicken over top. Sprinkle evenly with red pepper, green pepper and onion. Cover pizza with cheese. Bake for 10 to 12 minutes, or until cheese is melted.

"All jobs are easy to
the person who doesn't
have to do them."
~Anonymous~

BLT Cheese Wraps

1 lb. thick sliced bacon,
  cut into 1″ pieces
4 (12″) flour tortillas
1 C. shredded
  Cheddar cheese

½ head iceberg
  lettuce, shredded
1 tomato, diced

In a large, deep skillet over medium high heat, cook bacon pieces until evenly browned. Drain and set aside. Place 1 tortilla on a microwave-safe plate. Sprinkle tortilla with ¼ cup Cheddar cheese. Cook in microwave for 1 to 2 minutes, or until cheese is melted. Immediately top with ¼ of the bacon, lettuce and tomato. Fold sides of tortilla over, then roll up. Repeat with remaining ingredients. Cut each wrap in half before serving.

Breaded Turkey Breasts

1 C. bread crumbs
¼ C. grated
    Parmesan cheese
2 tsp. Italian seasoning
1 C. milk

1 lb. skinless, boneless
    turkey breasts,
    cut into strips
¼ C. olive oil

In shallow bowl, combine bread crumbs, Parmesan cheese and Italian seasoning. Into another shallow bowl, pour milk. Dip turkey strips in milk, then in crumb mixture. In a large skillet over medium heat, warm olive oil. Add turkey strips and cook for 8 to 10 minutes, or until golden brown and juices run clear.

Pesto Chicken Pizza

½ C. pesto basil sauce
1 (12″) pre-baked
  pizza crust
2 C. cooked chicken
  breast strips

1 (6 oz.) jar artichoke
  hearts, drained
½ C. shredded
  Fontina cheese

Preheat oven to 450°. Spread pesto sauce over pre-baked pizza crust. Arrange chicken strips and artichoke hearts over the sauce, and sprinkle with Fontina cheese. Bake for 8 to 10 minutes, or until Fontina cheese is melted and crust is lightly browned at the edges.

Grilled Italian Cheese

12 slices white bread
1 (8 oz.) pkg. shredded
 mozzarella cheese
¼ C. butter

⅛ tsp. garlic
 powder, optional
1 tsp. dried oregano
Marinara sauce

Preheat broiler. Place 6 slices of bread onto a baking sheet. Spread a small handful of the mozzarella cheese over each slice. Top with the remaining 6 slices of bread. In a small bowl, mix together the butter and garlic powder. Brush mixture over one side of the sandwiches, or spread with the back of a tablespoon. Sprinkle each sandwich with dried oregano over buttered side. Place baking sheet under the broiler for 2 to 3 minutes, until golden brown. Remove pan from oven, flip sandwiches, and brush the other sides with butter and sprinkle with oregano. Return to the broiler, and cook until golden, about 2 minutes. Cut sandwiches in half diagonally and serve immediately with marinara sauce on the side for dipping.

Italian Sausage Pepper and Onions

6 (4 oz.) links sweet
Italian sausage
2 T. butter
1 yellow onion, sliced
½ red onion, sliced
4 cloves garlic, minced

1 large red bell
pepper, sliced
1 green bell pepper, sliced
1 tsp. dried basil
1 tsp. dried oregano
¼ C. white wine

In a large skillet over medium heat, brown sweet Italian sausage on all sides. Remove from skillet and slice. In the same skillet, melt butter. Stir in the sliced yellow onion, red onion and garlic. Cook for 2 to 3 minutes, or until onions are slightly tender. Mix in red bell pepper and green bell pepper. Season with dried basil and dried oregano. Stir in white wine. Continue to cook and stir until peppers and onions are tender. Add sausage slices to skillet with the vegetables. Reduce heat to low, cover and simmer for 15 minutes, or until sausage is heated throughout.

Turkey Stroganoff

1 (8 oz.) pkg. uncooked
  egg noodles
1 T. vegetable oil
1 lb. ground turkey
1 T. minced onion
1 cube chicken
  bouillon, crumbled

1 (10¾ oz.) can cream
  of mushroom soup
½ C. water
1 T. paprika
Salt to taste

In a medium pot, boil egg noodles in 6 cups of lightly salted water, until noodles are al dente and drain. In a medium skillet over medium heat, warm vegetable oil. Add turkey and onion and cook until turkey is evenly browned and onion is tender. Mix in crumbled bouillon. Stir cream of mushroom soup and water into the skillet. Cook and stir until heated through. Season with paprika and salt to taste. Serve turkey mixture over the cooked egg noodles.

"Do the hard jobs first.
The easy jobs will take
care of themselves."
~Dale Carnegie~

Taco Lasagna

1 lb. ground beef
1 (1 oz.) pkg.
 taco seasoning
1 (14 oz.) can peeled and
 diced tomatoes in juice

10 (6″) corn
 tortillas, divided
1 C. salsa
½ C. shredded
 Colby cheese

Preheat oven to 350°. In a large skillet over medium high heat, brown ground beef. Stir in taco seasoning and tomatoes in juice. Line a 9 x 13″ baking dish with half of the tortillas. Spoon the beef mixture into the dish, then top with the remaining tortillas. Spread salsa over the tortillas and sprinkle with the cheese. Bake for 20 to 30 minutes, or until cheese is melted and bubbly.

Zucchini and Cheese

2 T. butter
1 large zucchini, chopped
1 large white
  onion, chopped
4 tomatoes, chopped

1 large green bell
  pepper, chopped
Italian seasoning to taste
1 (8 oz.) pkg. shredded
  mozzarella cheese

Preheat oven to 350°. Lightly grease a 9 x 13″ dish. In a medium skillet over medium heat, melt butter. Stir in zucchini and onion. Cook for 5 minutes, or until onion is golden brown. In the prepared casserole dish, mix the cooked zucchini, onion, tomatoes and green pepper. Season mixture with Italian seasoning and top with shredded cheese. Bake for 25 minutes, or until cheese is melted and bubbly.

Tomato Cucumber Salad

1 tomato
½ cucumber, peeled
1 C. mayonnaise

¼ C. sour cream
Dillweed to taste

Dice tomato and cucumber into small cubes. In a medium bowl, combine tomato, cucumber, mayonnaise and dillweed to taste. Chill in the refrigerator for at least 45 minutes before serving.

Super Easy Pasta Salad

1 lb. cooked spaghetti
1 (8 oz.) bottle
   Italian dressing
4 T. salad
   supreme seasoning

1 C. chopped tomatoes
1 C. chopped cucumbers

In a large bowl, combine cooked spaghetti, Italian dressing, salad supreme seasoning, chopped tomatoes and chopped cucumbers. Toss to coat evenly and serve.

"Anyone who uses the phrase
'easy as taking candy from a
baby' has never tried taking
candy from a baby."
~Unknown~

Carefree Crab Salad

1 head Romaine lettuce
1 small red onion, sliced
¾ lb. imitation crab meat

½ C. crumbled Feta cheese
1 (12 oz.) bottle olive oil
  vinaigrette dressing

Break Romaine lettuce into a salad bowl. Add onion to the lettuce. Crumble imitation crab meat and Feta cheese into the bowl. Top with olive oil vinaigrette dressing and toss to coat.

Fruit Cocktail Salad

1 (8¼ oz.) can fruit
  cocktail, drained
1 (11 oz.) can mandarin
  oranges, drained
1 (20 oz.) can pineapple
  chunks, drained
½ C. miniature
  marshmallows

2 T. lemon juice
1 (3 oz.) pkg. instant
  lemon pudding mix
2 bananas, peeled
  and sliced
2 C. whipped topping

In a medium bowl, combine drained fruit cocktail, drained mandarin oranges, drained pineapple chunks, marshmallows, instant lemon pudding mix and sliced bananas. Top with whipped topping and serve.

Eight Layer Salad

1 (5¼ oz.) pkg.
  scalloped potatoes
4 C. water, divided
½ C. Thousand
  Island dressing
¼ C. sour cream
4 C. shredded lettuce
1 C. sliced carrots

1 C. thinly sliced celery
1 small onion, thinly sliced
1 (10 oz.) pkg. frozen green
  peas, thawed and drained
½ C. shredded
  Cheddar cheese
4 slices bacon, crisply
  cooked and crumbled

In a 2½-quart pot over medium high heat, boil potatoes in 3 cups water. Reduce heat, cover and simmer until tender, about 15 to 20 minutes. Rinse potatoes under running cold water, drain and set aside. In the same pot over medium heat, boil remaining 1 cup water and seasoning mix from scalloped potatoes, stirring constantly. Stir in Thousand Island dressing and sour cream. In a medium bowl, combine sauce mixture and potatoes. Layer lettuce, carrots, celery, onion, peas, potato mixture, cheese and bacon in a serving bowl. Cover and refrigerate at least 8 hours. Serve with additional Thousand Island dressing, if desired.

Frozen Fruit Salad

1 (8 oz.) pkg. cream
  cheese, softened
¾ C. sugar
1 (20 oz.) can crushed
  pineapple, drained
1 (10 oz.) pkg.
  frozen strawberries

2 bananas, peeled
  and diced
1 (8 oz.) container
  whipped topping

In a medium bowl, stir cream cheese to soften and stir in sugar. Add drained pineapple, strawberries, bananas and whipped topping. Fold together and freeze. Remove from freezer and thaw for 10 minutes before cutting into slices to serve.

Summer Pea Salad

1 (10 oz.) bag frozen
  peas, uncooked
½ lb. cubed cheese,
  any kind
¼ C. bacon bits

¼ C. minced onion
1 tsp. sugar
2 C. mayonnaise

In a large bowl, mix frozen peas, cubed cheese, bacon pieces, minced onion, sugar and mayonnaise. Chill in the refrigerator before serving.

No Trouble Taco Salad

1 lb. ground beef
4 tomatoes, chopped
1½ C. shredded
   Cheddar cheese
1 head lettuce, shredded

1 pkg. taco seasoning
2 C. cheese flavored
   tortilla chips
1 (9 oz.) bottle Western or
   Catalina dressing

In a medium skillet over medium high heat, brown ground beef. In a medium bowl, mix cooked ground beef, chopped tomatoes, cheese, shredded lettuce and taco seasoning. Chill in the refrigerator for 10 to 15 minutes. Crumble cheese flavored tortilla chips over top of the salad just before serving.

Bacon Broccoli Salad

2 large stalks fresh broccoli
1 small bunch green onions
2 C. shredded Monterey
  Jack cheese

¼ C. bacon bits
1 (12 oz.) jar cole
  slaw dressing

In a medium bowl, break broccoli into bite size florets and chop green onion finely. Mix broccoli and green onions with cheese, bacon bits and cole slaw dressing. Toss to coat evenly. Cover bowl tightly and chill in refrigerator for 2 hours or overnight. Toss just before serving. Garnish with additional bacon bits, if desired.

"There's no easy way out.
If there were, I would
have bought it.
And believe me,
it would be one
of my favorite things!"
~Oprah Winfrey~

Easy Appetizers

Elegant Tomato Cheese Appetizer

4 tomatoes
1 lb. mozzarella cheese
2 T. olive oil
2 to 3 cloves garlic, minced

Salt and pepper to taste
Fresh basil
1 loaf Italian bread, sliced

Cut tomatoes and cheese into ¼″ slices. Layer tomato and cheese slices on platter or individual salad plates. Drizzle olive oil over top. Sprinkle with minced garlic, salt and pepper to taste. Garnish with fresh basil. Serve as topping for Italian bread slices.

Cream Cheese Crab Brick

1 (8 oz.) pkg. cream
   cheese, softened
1 (12 oz.) bottle chili sauce

1 (6 oz.) can fresh or
   imitation crab meat
Various crackers

Remove cream cheese from package and place whole on a platter. Cover with chili sauce and top with chunks of crab meat. Serve with crackers for dipping.

Basic Salami Breadsticks

½ lb. sliced Genoa salami
1 (16 oz.) pkg. whipped
  cream cheese
Garlic powder to taste

1 pkg. small sesame
  bread sticks

Spread 1 side of each slice of salami with cream cheese. Sprinkle desired amount of garlic powder over cheese. Place 1 bread stick at the end of 1 salami slice. Roll salami around bread stick. Repeat with remaining ingredients. Arrange appetizers on tray before serving.

Greek Cheese Appetizer

2 C. biscuit baking mix
1 C. buttermilk
2 eggs

½ C. butter, melted
2 C. crumbled Feta cheese
½ tsp. salt, optional

Preheat oven to 350°. In a medium bowl, mix together biscuit baking mix, buttermilk and eggs. Spread mixture on a greased baking sheet. Drizzle melted butter over mixture and sprinkle with Feta cheese and salt. Bake for 35 to 40 minutes. Remove from oven and let cool for 10 minutes. Cut into bite size pieces and serve.

Lemon Whip

2 eggs, beaten
Juice of 1½ lemons
1 C. sugar

1 C. heavy whipping cream
½ C. graham
   cracker crumbs

In a double boiler over boiling water, combine eggs, lemon juice and sugar, mixing until thick. Allow to cool. Using an electric mixer, whip 1 cup heavy cream until soft peaks form. Fold whipped cream into the lemon mixture. Cover the bottom of a shallow 8″ square glass baking dish with graham cracker crumbs. Spread the lemon mixture over graham cracker crumbs. Chill in refrigerator until ready to serve.

Chocolate Dream

1 (18 oz.) box chocolate
  cake mix
2 (4 oz.) pkg. chocolate
  instant pudding

1 (21 oz.) can
  cherry pie filling
2 (8 oz.) containers
  whipped topping

In a 9 x 13″ pan, prepare cake mix according to directions on box and bake in oven. Let cake completely cool. In a medium bowl, prepare pudding mix according to directions on package. Cut chocolate cake into 2″ squares. In separate dessert bowls, lay down one cake square and top with some of the chocolate pudding, then cherry pie filling, then whipped topping. Repeat with all cake squares.

Angel Food Fluff

1 (10 oz.) prepared
   angel food cake
1 (14 oz.) can sweetened
   condensed milk
2 lemons

2 C. heavy
   whipping cream
½ C. sugar
Shredded
   coconut, optional

Cut angel food cake into small pieces. Using an electric mixer, whip the sweetened condensed milk and add the juice of both lemons. In a separate bowl, beat together heavy whipping cream and sugar until soft peaks form. Fold whipped cream into the pudding mixture. Transfer mixture to a serving bowl. Layer angel food pieces over mixture. Top with shredded coconut, if desired.

Simple Stuffed Strawberries

1 pint fresh strawberries
1 (8 oz.) pkg. cream
   cheese, softened

½ C. powdered sugar
2 T. orange flavored liqueur

Cut tops off strawberries and stand upright, cut-side-down. In each strawberry, cut a slit ¾ of the way down from the tip of the strawberry towards the bottom. In a medium bowl, using an electric mixer, beat together cream cheese, powdered sugar and orange liqueur until smooth. Transfer cream cheese mixture into a piping bag with a star tip. Pipe cream cheese mixture into the slit in each strawberry. Arrange stuffed strawberries on a platter and serve.

Index

Fast Recipes

Fast Main Dishes

Curried Chicken Soup 8
Fab Fettuccine with Creamy Ham Sauce...................... 15
Fast Chicken Fettuccine... 5
Garbanzo Beans and Couscous 3
Ginger Dill Fish Fillets.. 10
Manageable Microwave Meatloaf................................... 17
Microwave Cheesy Potato Soup 12
Pork BBQ 4
Quick Lasagna Casserole.. 11
Shrimp Casserole... 13
Single Shepherd's Pies 14
Speedy Sausage and Beans 6
Spiced Chicken 16
Sweet Sesame Chicken Kabob Salad 9
Tangy Dinner Steaks 7
Tasty Thai Noodles and Shrimp 2

Fast Side Dishes

Apricot Acorn Squash.. 21
Asian-Style Zucchini... 19
Bacon Baked Beans 22
Balsamic Bow Tie Pasta 32
Balsamic Carrots.. 24
Brisk Baked Pineapple 23
Broccoli Salad.. 29
Candied Acorn Squash 25
Creamy Peas 26
Field Salad 30
Green Beans and Almonds.. 18
Lovely Lemon Pepper Pasta 27
Parmesan Asparagus... 20
Snappy Fruit Salad.. 31
Sunflower Seed and Apple Salad 28

Fast Appetizers

Bacon Blanket Water Chestnuts 34
Piping Hot Ponderosas 33
Sesame Chicken Nuggets... 35

Fast Desserts

Caramel Banana Fluff 37
Chocolate Éclair... 39
Cup of Cheese Cake 38
Dashing Apple Delight 36
Dessert Crepes 40

Cheap Recipes
Cheap Main Dishes

BBQ Beef Cups 53
Bacon Potato Soup 55
Budget Beef Stroganoff 45
Cheap and Easy Chicken... 46
Chicken and Vegetables... 51
Classic Corn Dogs.. 54
Creamy Round Steak and Potatoes 48
Crock Pot Tuna Casserole 56
Easy Oriental Dinner 49
French Onion Soup 58
Gee Whiz Cheesy Chicken Casserole.................................... 44
Pumpkin Nut Soup.. 57
Ranch Chicken Casserole.. 42
Reasonable Roast... 47
Simple Tator Tot Casserole 52
Spicy Baked Fish 50
Three Bean Casserole 43

Cheap Side Dishes

Apple Yam Casserole.. 59
Baked Mac and Cheese.. 64
Cheese Potatoes 61
Chili Cheese Cornbread 60
Chili Tots 62
Corn Chip Salad 67

Fruity Cole Slaw... 69
Mashed Potatoes and Onions 66
Nutmeg Potatoes.. 65
Simple Macaroni Salad 63
Sweet Citrus Salad 68

Cheap Appetizers
Asparagus Wraps.. 71
Bacon Onion Wheels 72
Broiled Cheesy Potato Skins 73
Tofu Taco Dip 70

Cheap Desserts
Berry Berry Parfaits 78
Blender Chocolate Mousse.. 80
Chocolate Crisps... 77
Microwave Peanut Brittle 74
Minute Cookies 79
Peppermint Kisses 75
Strawberry Rice Pudding 76

Easy Recipes

Easy Main Dishes
American-Style Chop Suey 89
BLT Cheese Wraps 94
BLAT 91
Baked Bean Sandwiches 92
Baked Chicken Breasts with Worcestershire 85
Barbecue Chicken Pizza 93
Basic Chicken Parmesan 83
Breaded Turkey Breasts 95
Creamy Cheese Chicken... 102
Curry Apple Turkey Pita.. 90
Grilled Italian Cheese 97
Italian Sausage Pepper and Onions.................................... 98
Italian-Style Baked Eggs 86
Laid Back Lemon Garlic Chicken 84
Parmesan-Crusted Chicken... 87
Pesto Chicken Pizza 96

Rice Wreck.. 101
Simple Chicken and Rice... 82
Sunshine Sandwich 93
Sweet Pea Mint Soup.. 88
Taco Lasagna 100
Turkey Stroganoff... 99

Easy Sides

Bacon Broccoli Salad... 112
Carefree Crab Salad... 106
Eight Layer Salad 108
Frozen Fruit Salad 109
Fruit Cocktail Salad... 107
No Trouble Taco Salad... 111
Summer Pea Salad 110
Super Easy Pasta Salad 105
Tomato Cucumber Salad 104
Zucchini and Cheese.. 103

Easy Appetizers

Basic Salami Breadsticks.. 115
Cream Cheese Crab Brick 114
Elegant Tomato Cheese Appetizer 113
Greek Cheese Appetizer 116

Easy Desserts

Angel Food Fluff.. 119
Chocolate Dream... 118
Lemon Whip 117
Simple Stuffed Strawberries 120